GW01395841

PAINTING THE VESTIBULE

Betty Thompson

for Uta

with best wishes

Betty Thompson

scalltamedia

for
Jim Thompson

Published in 2009 by
Scallta Media,
34, Weafer Street, Enniscorthy,
Co Wexford, Ireland.
W: www.scalltamedia.com
E: info@scalltamedia.com

Copyright © Betty Thompson 2009

ISBN 978-0-9563710-0-3

All rights reserved. No part of this publication may be reproduced
or transmitted in any form or by any means, electronic or mechani-
cal, including photography, recording, or any information storage
or retrieval system, without permission in writing from the pub-
lisher. The book is sold subject to the condition that it shall not, by
way of trade or otherwise, be lent, resold, or otherwise circulated
without the publisher's prior consent in any form of binding or cover
other than that in which it is published and without a similar con-
dition, including this condition, being imposed on the subsequent
purchaser.

Cover photo by Anni Cullen

Cover design and typesetting by Paul O'Reilly

Printed in Ireland by Colour Books

scalltamedia

Among the high-branching, leafless boughs
Above the roof-peaks of the town,
Snowflakes unnumberably come down.

HOWARD NEMEROV

Acknowledgments

Some of the poems have been broadcast on RTÉ Radio or appeared in the following publications: *Coffee House Poetry, Envoi, The Scaldy Detail, Crannóg* and *The SHOp*.

Contents

Curlew at Bull Island

My bill describes a curve
the shape of searching.

I come alone to the water's edge,
keep my distance
from that frill of dunlin,
the patch of ringed plover.

Others too wait for this time.
They stake out our ground,
turn their lenses on us.
Some stare through slits in huts.

Inland on the promenade,
under the windblown cordylines,
some brightly marked ones are running.
Drab ones walk, leading dogs.

A man stops to gaze at me
across marram grasses, mud, the receding tide.

Looking for the Westin Hotel

Two streets, cut parallel, slipping out
from College Green, making for the Liffey.

At the Ulster Bank, opposite the long stretching
one at Foster Place – dim stone cul-de-sac,
sombre street, mouth of a gallery,
 a cool, cobbled close we cross but seldom enter –
you asked the way to the Westin Hotel.

D'Olier Street, Westmoreland Street –
it was one or the other, I said,
neither is far from here.

But still you stood there, waiting
to be convinced, I thought, about the location
of the Westin Hotel, uneasy that I gave a choice,
seemed uncertain perhaps or blasé about
those streets, their stone,
the shadows they cast towards dusk,
a great newspaper housed in one,
the languor of an oriental café,
a chiselled prow at the ballast office -
and somewhere in the middle, I knew,
without ever looking down after
that first startling glance,
a sculptor's shimmering footprints.

The backing away was good, in a way,
taking you in the direction of the Westin Hotel,
yet an odd, anachronistic movement, like the exit of a courtier -
except your head was high, level with mine,
and you looked me in the eye and then came closer.

Elegy for Donal McCann

1

One night on Jones's Road,
on the terrace of houses below the road,
he opened a window and slipped in.

'No-one heard me at the door,'
he said later,
'so I had to try a window.'

Undeterred by the dimness and silence on that doorstep,
determined not to disappoint his hostess, her guests,
he hopped up on the windowsill,
grasped the lower sash and pushed.

2

One night on Usher's Island he went to a party.
It was the right night.
It was snowing.
It was Twelfth Night, the night for visits.
It was snowing.

His aunts fretted at his lateness,
feared he would not come.
They came out onto the landing,
closing out the notes of a polonaise,
to listen for the footfall of horses, their harness.

Snow
settled on the shoulders of his overcoat,
stiffened the spaces in its buttonholes.

15

He had to scrape it from his galoshes
on the mat in the hall.
Then he gave the maid a gold coin.
It was the night for gifts.

Later, he sits out a waltz -
his lithe form charged with breath,
his head full of some chafing, puzzling guilt,
an insult hurled at him in the dance.

Beside him, a mother frets:
'Is Freddy all right?'
'He's nearly all right,' he says, remembering
her son's rich breath, uncertain gait,
the tremulous voice edging towards fracture.

Gérard Depardieu in Eustace Street

His fleshy face aslant fills the screen
here in this vaulted room
still light enough to see the patina on oak
though the lights are down
as I sit in a plush row where benches used to seat
the friends who met here
in silence mostly
unless one felt impelled to speak about the light within.

We too sit in silence
looking up at the screen of light
receiving its forms and tints
tracking their force
tasting the full mouthed vowels and moist consonants
of its habitués this day
 who
inhabiting or sojourning in the drab part of town
relocate for a scene or two
to its volcanic hinterland
to daze themselves with light and air.

Cream

I'm whipping cream with a balloon whisk
out on the verandah.
Across the grassy fronts, our mingled lawns,
a girl hurls a ball to her dad:
it arcs, she strikes the air and spins.
This is how they play.
I whisk slack cream, fill it with air.
As darkness falls, the hurl brightens.
The cream lightens in my bowl, the whisk slows.

The Sculptor

i.m. Barbara Hepworth

Afternoons, she'd go with him on his rounds -
rising and falling with the hill shapes,
driving up to brows,
bending into curves,
rolling over plateaux.

Somewhere in the middle of her body she mapped it -
shading its heights,
greening its depths,
ears swelling on the climb,
then a shiver on the breast.

It undulated on her back,
dipped under her arms, finding pools and lakes.

Its streams coursed down her arms.
.

Learning to be I
(after Antony Gormley at Lismore)

Thick trunks and throats,
fronding branches –

a giant *corps de ballet* parting
to show in a pool of light -
wood rib, tree slice, man trunk.

He's on toe-tip.

I stand with him
on a woodland floor
shaded by trees whose shadows
lie across it like a ladder.

Beyond them, framed by
spindle trunks, leaf swags -
light on a sloping lawn.

Wrapt
(after Eilis O'Connell at Lismore)

mouth of a cave
slender egg narrowing
the space a boat takes up in the sea   *or*
leaves on the sand when it is launched

leaf dust speckles
a gathering arm

sleep in it hide in it
I could slip
or sway   *or even*
fall in it

                    still
I would be held

                    amid

veins of blue and turquoise
crackles of taupe shimmering to gold

Ludwig's Gifts

(after Harry Clarke's window at Sturminster Newton)

Gloves

I bring gloves to guard your fingers
from our harsh northern winters
when snow settles on the tips of my father's firs,
when paths glisten with ice.

Let their weft nudge the down of your skin,
let the cuffs caress your forearms.

Yet draw them taut
so the seams curve up where the skin thins
and a new finger begins.

Coral Rosary

How deep did sailors dive
so you could bring these beads?

Did they strike with force and axe
or break it where they would, like nougat?

And did you know when you gave me this garland -
which even now entwines my fingers like honeysuckle,
whose silver chain glints in the starlight,
its links etching crescents onto my skin -
that I would chant these decades for you?

Eleanor

The President, your husband, tested you
for years, doling out love amongst women.
Flawed promise-breaker (one among many)
yet some goodness, more than allure, held you.
Buffed brittle you shone, and would not break.
You wove his care into your world.

So the lives run, yours and his, full
till some soreness, some clear knowing, weights you,
draws you those days to Rock Creek, its graves,
the holly grove and bronze monument to
Clover who, making images with light,
finding her life dark, ended it.

Holly - exquisite leaf-tips pierce, blood-red berries feed -
you sit in a ring of it, devotee of grief, visiting your own.
You brought Hick here on the eve of his triumph.
Not defiant, no, nor to show her a wound salved,
but to know that here in this city where men and power surge
all these things can be pondered in the heart.

Elegy for Blanche de la Force

(among the Carmelites of Compiègne guillotined 17th July 1794)

The horses pulled up short.
Men in caps shook the carriage.
Your mother fell and he held her in his arms.
The men looked in and leered.

In your father's house that night –

   your birth screams
    her death cries.

Then all those years
motherless,
fearful.

You sought one in the Abbey
when it was time to leave your father's house.
She too was dying when you met her
and full of terror.
Welcome daughter, she said.

Later, when men stormed the Abbey, you ran.
Another found you in your father's house.
You called out that the stew burned.
The smell is everywhere, you cried.
She poured it into a clean dish.
This is fit to eat, she said.

Was this the act that drew you back to your sisters?
(for amongst sisters the mother cannot be distant,
their presence evokes her.)
Did you feel safe then,

free to voice the last note
in that diminishing choir?

Garden at Charleston, East Sussex

Here at the wall –

beside the berry clusters,
sun on my shoulders –

a bee enters the bowl of a flower,
pale pink frills streaked to its heart, chick yellow -

chooses it over lush reds, maroons and mauves,
velvet sepals, arching stems, rose hips.

Sweet peas reach to a swag of foliage,
twine merges with stems, the pergola sags –
amongst them all a web shines.

The house is never out of my sight –
its windows, doors, chimneys,
the lawn rising to it.

Ballet painting on wood
(after Duncan Grant at Charleston)

He burned the last logs last night -
didn't see the splinters in corners,
wood dust settling into my seams.

The ashes were warm when he came
and would have sparked if he'd stirred them.
But it was me he wanted, not my burden.

He carried me through the house,
out of my element into his.
My riches lie inside, I wanted to cry,
my freight warms your flesh, you cherish it.

A panel drenched with colour -
contours of hips, calves, high Russian cheekbones,
calligraphy of reach and gaze,
the grace of flesh filling it.

Lake George Georgia O'Keeffe

After the flower pictures -
their curves and sinews,
fleshy pinks and bruised purples -
land stops and water begins -
water held in land, pulling me to its shore.
I swim up the lily cone
shimmying over its lip.

Magdalene reading

I knew the children were not at school
because it was a holiday
but when I checked the rooms
they were empty.

'They're all right,' she says, when I ask,
'They went out with my sister.'

All around her on the table
are splayed spoons, shallow
pools of milk in cereal bowls.

They had toast too, I saw, from
its shimmering spray,
the dripped butter that had set
in the grooves of the table
on which she leans into her clearing,
from where she looks up at me
from her book.

To St Anthony emerging from a vision

(after Ana Maria Pacheco's triptych)

No blood yet
only the slack lips.
Howling has dried up your mouth,
scarred the lining of your throat.

The undertips of your toes
cling to the floor
like burrs.
A foot twists forward.

A man has thrust his arm
under yours
where it is hollow.
It presses into bone
at the edges of your armpit
and the arm hangs limp.

He has caught you,
that man with orange-red hair,
its tints leaching
into bodice and sleeve.

Louise Bourgeois at the Serpentine

Stuffed hose dangles from curved steel.
I cannot guess its denier
but note its fleshy pinkness,
a taut gusset at the toe.

Here, clothes-hangers are bones
whose knuckled ends trap shoulder straps.

A black sheath, devoré,
winds round a fleshy pole.
A faceless figure, roughly stitched,
hangs from flexed steel wire.

People are staring in through the little
square panes at a plump copulating pair:
horizontally placed, mid-air,
an arm hooks the torso below.

Out at the lake, yards from this pavilion,
an angler casts his baited line.

In winter

the laden fire,
lights springing to the sky,
my gloved hand gripped fast,
toffee softening in my mouth.

I follow the path through the park.
I see you make a slide of ice,
smoothing it with your boot
like a restless horse.

Stopping in woods, Newton St Loe

Smooth beech laths fixed tautly –
but how they curve to meet the human shape!

I ordered the men to place it precisely here
where an accumulation of gradients
would have so impacted on the cardiovascular system
that the family and their guests would stop and rest.

Evenings, I came here while they dined.
I didn't need the meshed woodland at my back
to feel secure.   The slanting verdure at my feet,
bathing my opening eyes, I could take or leave.

A rash of splinters infects this timber –
the laths are sprung apart.
The woody spikes will tear the flesh of all
who might seek rest here –
yet guard the ascending forest, the dropping glade.

Piano shop, Manchester

No one passes without glancing into
those long plain windows, floor

to ceiling high, stretching the length
of my long hotel, from where

I look out from my top-storey room,
elbows on the sill. No one sees me

here on my perch above
the thinning traffic, above

the street lamps, though the light
that draws me is from fluorescent strips,

halogen spots and who knows
how many hidden sources, flooding

the glazed cubes, causing
passers-by to slow or even stop

to gaze at grand pianos, parallelograms
of dull walnut or watery white casing

squinting in the light, lids raised,
as if to say, here are tone and resonance freed.

Sound

When that rude timpani began in the stillness
I thought a hubcap had popped off a wheel,
gone rolling down the street,
rising and falling like a dancer's skirt,
stopping on the circle it covered -

or that out in the garden
the bin lid, out of kilter,
its generous rim askew on the drum,
careened down the steps till it hit a wall -

or that down in the pantry someone,
sneaking among long cool shelves,
brushing against a jelly mould,
sent it hopping and spinning on the tiles below
where its tinny hollows resonate.

Worm

In these passages
warmed by boiler and stove,
fed by morsels of crumb
and spatters of fat from
lamb grilling on a trivet

the worm grew and swelled.

Today it dares to reveal itself,
to dive from its hard pine pocket
where steel blades slid beside its skin:
a chameleon lands on
the slubbed mock-marble worktop.

I bring the insect trap -
perspex, domed, a sliding door
from a magician's trick-box.

Outside, released into the winter bed,
beneath a canopy of rose leaves,
rosemary branches, fading pink lacecaps,
it coils round a laurel stem.

Golden Ash

All winter I worried about the ash.
I'd seen the sap holding its own
but the short brittle ends of branches,
their ghosts of leaves, played on my mind.

One morning my neighbour crossed the lawn.
Is that tree dead, she asked.

I pointed to the cuts I'd made in the bark –
we stooped to look at little green dashes
on the pale stem.

Valentine

I went to the Christmas drawer to find it –
that deep, creaking drawer under the wardrobe
where we store decorations for cakes and walls,
cotton snowmen and baubles for the tree.
Sheets of tissue – red, pink and gold –
lay wrapped in brown paper.

I chose the red tissue,
sat down on the faded rug in that room
and reached for my scissors.

Look, I have made you a rose –
plucked translucent petals two by two
from the taut centre of a paper fold.

Cherry Blossom, Northumberland Road

Petals drift from the limbs of a tree,
a pink span of early summer.

Your hand opens in explication, fingers
catch the fall of blossom, and we

could not ignore the touch of petals
on your skin, their scent, as if the impact

when you raised your hand so
minimally, of fingertip on petal, was enough

to press out their scent, drawing my eyes
to the little silken ovals, especially

those you caught, held momentarily,
then let fall or lobbed into the air

a fraction of an inch above your rising
hand, or to its side, while the breeze sent

more in a slow shower, patterning
the air, your shoulders, the books we held.

Leaves after Rain

Leaves from the birch lay in mounds.
Rain, the tramp of builders' boots, the sure
pad of my neighbour's cat, had not moved them.

A large spoonful of leaves, damp and limp,
lay snug in a corner where steps
edge the heather bed.

I nudged them with the toe of my shoe,
spreading the tawny mass to let the breeze
restore their crackle.

Strand

Wind a ruff round my neck,
wet sand,
flounces on waves.

Ahead a little sandbar -
low like the waves,
long and plump like a new grave.

In amongst the dunes
low sprays of sand
rise in my wake.

Further out, in tight packed curving rills,
like a long, flung, undulating scarf,
the sand is slick and bouncy.

Somewhere along the shoreline
I give in to the sea,
stand on the rim of its flow.

Miles to the north two fishing boats sit on the horizon
drained of depth
like a child's drawing.

Flight

Clouds drift, curl, fragment.
Wisps float, dissolve till
there are no more glimpses
of the height we've climbed,
the air between us and land,
only the shimmer of white.
Midway it's like the sea, all waves and ripples.
Like the sea gone wild with bands of water
facing each other, moving in a ghostly minuet
where dancers, intimate and aloof,
stir the shared atmosphere.
Now the ocean is scooped into suites
whose doors open and close over and over
making the waters rush and recede.

Ingress

When a half Roman tile shifted
in a summer storm, the rain washed in.
It soaked the roof felt till it sagged and tore,
making a place for water to enter the walls.

Peeling back the paper, I see a rough mottled patch -
dull creams, beiges, bleached-out parchment,
pinks bleeding to scalloped russet edges,
like a manuscript someone has tried to burn.

Inside lane

Not knowing when night will fall,
at twilight I take the inside lane,
knowing that now the traffic lightens
and walkers have reached home.

Down here in the inside lane,
taking up a bike width, watching
for beams of headlights from the rear,
listening for ascending engines,
I'm ready to step up momentarily,
out of the way of a car at my back
just long enough to let it to pass.
Then I'm down again in my lane
more than an arm's length away
from the mouth of that dark lane,
from the fuzzy green body of a pittosoporum
spilling out through a gap in the fence.

Even if, more than an arm's length away,
the sound of footsteps on this asphalt road
or the exhalations from my tightened throat
were heard in the mouth of that lane,
in the lee of that bush, I,
being more than an arm's length away,
can keep my place.

Painting the vestibule

Through thin sandals
the grip of ribbed steel -
a splayed ladder fills this little room.

I can make bold strikes on the cornice,
dab into ridges, the crevices near carved leaves,
dismount when the stretch is too far
to turn and turn.

Even if the rubber fails to hold and I skid,
if the shelf leaves its fixings and it folds, collapses –
the walls will hold me.

But that day in the manège,
the horse going round and round,
its reins tight in my hands –

a girl pays out the lunge, backs to the centre.
Round we go, the horse and I, round and round,
the reins looser, the lunge longer.

Art Exhibition:
'The Martello Tower, Sandycove'

Standing on his tower,
the French woman at my elbow says,
is like standing on a ship.

So, Joyce, gazing out from the parapet,
dreaming of skimming the wine-dark sea,
going home to Ithaca, wife and son,
squints and gasps as the great aqueous expanse
shrinks, sloshes and splashes ashore
into gutters, drains, horse-troughs, fountains, holy water
fonts,
the beds of rivers, visible and invisible.

Liffey Patrol

Down here the river looks wide like the sea,
but it can't be the sea - look at those walls -
the skeins of knobbly scum appliquéd on stone.

I patrol the river, circling my patch,
steering towards other boats,
halting just before they must.

'Why me?' one of them says,
'just because you're boss?'
I stare, then veer to his right.

My vessel has bounce and grace.
I ride the green waves.

Liffey Swell

High tide and thick green waves
slap around pilasters,
push mortar from the spaces
between limestone slabs
till they shift and tumble into the water,
pull down the carved faces of river gods,
cause people on the bridge to fall –

> those traders with open cases
> like shallow quilted wardrobes
> holding bronze and leather bracelets
> etched with girls' names

(the loops of thonging, russet and purple,
to weave through braided hair,
might unfurl and float)

> tourists with maps and tans, neat rucksacks,
> locals with shopping bags –

all drop into the risen water.

Those who can, swim to the ladders,
grab and climb, smell the silted stone,
while up on the quays we watch and scream
as water heaves against the walls,
trapping trunks and limbs,
dragging them into its cold, slimy wetness
where the city's debris steeps.

Years ago a piano, no longer upright,

its walnut casing bobbing on the waves,
was sighted near the bridge at Church Street
and hauled up with ropes.

And once, at low tide, a man saw a cat on the river-bed,
yards below the quay, waiting to drown,
making no move to catch the nearby rungs
with her pads or claws.

Now divers, broad in their rubber suits,
throw down rafts, drop dinghies, retrieve
swimmers, floaters, bodies of the dead.

The Forty Steps

curve through this wall
ancient guard

a ghost clings to
the dank innards

a grey floating dripping
long-fingered thing

it might snarl or gnaw at me
chase and catch me

unable to raise my knee
halfway where no light enters

so the fear soaks in
of the ghost in the steps

or the ghosts of men
who lean at nearby corners

that one who staggers
in odorous clothes

whose voice shifts
between songs and curses

Church at Sandymount

where the road swerves
into Sandymount
a heavy ball
swings

stones
split   shift   fall

dust
ascends

clogs the breath-channels
of passers-by

who startled
see crumble

a sober worship place
a shape against the sky

hillocks of debris
succeed
the street mark of summer walks
the darkening stone
glimpsed from a rain-spattered bus

when the scene revives

it's not the engine's
growl
the clang of metal on stone

that ring in my ear

it's the sound of someone
fumbling in a till

The Dig

Fishamble Street:
a boomerang that was never thrown or returned
but kept its place, its scissor-shape -
      finger and thumb in silver rings
      make skin and tendon stretch
      and the tapering blades glint -

a window glows ochre.
Tart apples dipped in toffee
bring children ribboning in.
Pennies clink on the counter.
Oil burns, burns.
Oozes into light.

At a village fete,
amid cottages, wisteria,
within sight of the maypole, its streamers -
a beekeeper shows his hive behind glass.
I dare to face it -
the teeming comb,
bees spinning their thick sweetness.

Today I stand at a locked gate.
Low strings of bunting mark the pit,
little flags of colour like strips of paper dolls.
Rows of workers stoop
to humps and mats of wattle and daub,
its pale weave calming
the yellow sheen of their helmets.

Homes

-Listen, why don't you write about us,
the new dispossessed, the ones who couldn't
make a home in their bit of the city?
It's that Celtic Tiger again –
lithe, sated, greedy, regal and beautiful,
star of the city, the country, dazzling
Europe, the world, with its brassy radiance.
Here am I, on the far edge of my city,
clinging to the fringe of it, straining
to see the place I left, hearing new accents,
looking at different colours of brick.

-Listen, I know how you feel,
The memories and all that, but
it's not so bad.   It's not so far.
Make new memories.

She didn't say count your blessings -
might have meant it though, not knowing
I count, classify, process them in my brain,
construct with them a finely honed argument
to prove that I am blessed.
I express gratitude.
I make plans, calculate, place myself on
the grid of social and economic prosperity.
I draw mind maps and diagrams.
I look into my garden, at trees and
shrubs which have rooted and thrive.

In York Street they are demolishing old houses -
gracious once -

lately, beloved tenement homes.
No-one wanted to leave.
They made a promise to build them new homes
on the same plot of ground.
When they return to that spot on the map of their city,
will it be as if they had never left?

They left, holding the promise.

Good Friday on Merrion Road

An Indian man on a broad empty pavement.
An Indian man in pale clothes.
Can you tell me, he said, how to get to Bray?
Beside us, a bank behind railings.
In between the bank and the railings,
a grove of guarded saplings.
I think about crants,
those garlands brought to the funerals of girls
who had not lived to bear a wedding posy.
Flowers never thrown but caged in glass
to hang in mourning.

Sun slants on the Indian man's smile.
Traffic flows between us and the great mass of the RDS.
It was there that once a boy, hearing the sound of violins,
tugged on his mother's sleeve and said,
'I want to play that music'.
Today he strolls beside the Hudson, relishing its breadth,
its distance from that time.

I tell the Indian man about the bus to Bray.
Keep walking towards the city, I say,
and somewhere in the inner reaches of Hawkins Street
join the huddle of people waiting.

Chatterton's House

That day you saw a house –

not the same age as his, or in the same style,
not even in the same country -

but the same shape and volume,
taking up the same amount of ground and air,
set at the same angle to the road,
abutting it, turned inwards,
in the lee of the prevailing wind,
shaded by whatever trees can grow there,
its windows skewed from your line of vision.

Close up the windows are murky,
clouded with city grime, a skein of debris -
abandoned webs, collapsed nests,
blackened crevices, a spatter of motes.

Leaving Warsaw

Yet another woman hoeing
to nick and deaden weeds
so that florets, roots, leaves
can sprout, reach, thrive.

Further south the farms expand.
A single crop fills field after field,
the gauzy tops a froth of alliums.

And I am back at supper in a Warsaw flat
rubbing garlic onto dry toast -
our host's *plat de résistance*:
burnt gold and dull white slices side by side.

Juice seeps into bread.
Fingertips let fall
the grazed and pungent discs.

Lunchtime at Nussbaum & Wu

A girl is breaking a bagel over a mixed green salad
and reading *Revolutionary Road*.
Creamy pendant light bowls hover.
Turning a page, raising a forkful of spinach,
her arm brushes the sage wainscotting,
animates her image
in the huge eau-de-nil framed mirrors.
Ceiling fans whir like birds who have flown absentmindedly
into a garden room.

Ivy

for John McCarthy

Here, take this ivy:

its cream-fringed tessellated foliage,
trained to arch and dip through hooped wire,
springs pert and smooth from potted loam.

It could rest on the sill of a north-facing room
or, snug in a crazed Art Deco saucer,
perch on the corner of a slate hearth.

I gave your girl a plant and you came home:

a plant of shade and shelter.
She bore it shoulder-high through the stalls -
Its mossy pole,
stems falling into decades of leaves.

Courtyard

Shyly, he invited us to enter
the courtyard we had stopped outside,
gestured that we move towards the centre
where something gold had died.
The shallow beds were lush with giant leaves
that brushed the tiered piazzas of his home.
I thought I'd found a place of private ease
made langourous with foliage and stone.
He led us to an oval pond.
A goldfish lay curled
amid leaves on a half-sunken pot.
He said, we lost him in the cold.
I saw the tender way he lifted him
and placed his golden body on the rim.

Showing

Look, a tooth in the hand.
He wants to show it to me.
Rushes through the runners,
kickers, throwers, skippers,
shouters, screamers, chasers,
jumpers, strollers, sitters,
lone shufflers.
It just came out.   Creamy and grey,
trickle of blood.
Wrap it up, pocket it.
Sleep on it later.

Look, a poem in the hand.
He wants to show it to me.
Sidles out of nowhere.
It's finished now.   Creased jotter page,
lines and lines of pencil words.
Reads it out, pockets it.
Might unfold it later.

Seeing Angels

There seemed to be no space between their backs
and the walls as they levitated over the doorway,
its rendered planes –
yet they were in a kneeling pose,
hung there facing each other across the doorway,
framing it like a lych gate.
Such aplomb, to guard your threshold with angels!
Pale yellows and fawns, thickened balsa carved
to show the finest indentations of wing and tress.

Somewhere inside a door is ajar.
Light seeps through the fanlight.

Would that light, weak and steady,
have been enough to show them,
full length and full featured,
pleated draperies and closed lips,
as I drove by them that night?

Or did it need the glancing beam
from my headlamps to move through
griselinia leaves, holly berries,
the white trunks of birches,
before arching up to that brief dazzle?